Dump Dinners Family-Friendly Soup, Slow Cooker and Skillet Inspired by The Mediterranean Diet

by **Vesela Tabakova**
Text copyright(c)2015 Vesela Tabakova

Table Of Contents

Dump Dinners and Dishes –
Healthy Meal Ideas for When You're In a Hurry

We live in an age where everybody is constantly on the move and putting a home-cooked meal on the table during a busy weeknight can be more than challenging. But no matter how hectic your day is, it is really important that you take a moment and enjoy a good, hearty meal. Because while there may be more than one right way to eat, scientists agree on one thing – the more real, natural, unprocessed food you eat, the better. And I believe good nutrition is the best gift we can give ourselves and our loved ones.

While it may look and sound difficult to cook healthy, non-processed food at home, after trying out some of my dump dinners recipes, you will soon realize you can throw together a healthy family dinner in no time. All my Mediterranean diet inspired dump dinners ideas are super easy to prepare, and are excellent options to whip up on a weeknight. Simply prep a few healthy ingredients, toss them in a pot, skillet or slow cooker, and cook them together while you go about your busy life - it doesn't get any easier than that! When you come back, you have a healthy, aromatic meal that your family is certain to fall in love with.

Weeknight dinner ideas are hard to come by. For me, preparing delicious dump dinners is the easiest and most stress-free way of cooking fast, yet amazingly tasty good food for the family. My Mediterranean dump dinners recipes use simple ingredients that you probably already have on hand in your freezer, refrigerator, and pantry. They do not require complicated cooking techniques and are simply the best solution for fast-paced families who want tasty and healthy meals. At the end of a busy day, dump dinners are the perfect answer to the question, What's for dinner!

Mediterranean Chicken Soup

Serves 5-6

Ingredients:

1.5 lb chicken breasts, diced

3-4 carrots, chopped

1 celery rib, chopped

1 red onion, chopped

8 cups water

10 black olives, pitted and halved

1/2 tsp salt

ground black pepper, to taste

lemon juice, to serve

1/2 cup fresh parsley or coriander, finely cut, to serve

Directions:

Dump all ingredients in a soup pot. Stir well and bring to a boil. Reduce heat and simmer for 30-40 minutes.

Serve with lemon juice and sprinkled with fresh parsley or coriander.

Curried Lentil Soup

Serves 5-6

Ingredients:

1 cup dried lentils

1 large onion, finely cut

1 celery rib, chopped

1 large carrot, chopped

3 garlic cloves, chopped

1 can tomatoes, undrained

3 cups chicken broth

1 tbsp curry powder

1/2 tsp ground ginger

4 bacon slices, cooked and crumbled, to serve

Directions:

Combine all ingredients in slow cooker.

Cover and cook on low for 5-6 hours.

Blend soup to desired consistency, adding additional hot water to thin, if desired.

Serve topped with crumbled bacon.

Dump Bean and Bacon Soup

Serves 5-6

Ingredients:

1 slices bacon, chopped

1 can Black Beans, rinsed

1 can Kidney Beans, rinsed

1 celery rib, chopped

1/2 red onion, chopped

1 can tomatoes, diced, undrained

4 cups water

1 tsp smoked paprika

1 tsp dried mint

1/2 cup fresh parsley

ground black pepper, to taste

Directions:

Dump all ingredients in a soup pot. Stir well and bring to a boil. Reduce heat and simmer for 35 minutes.

Season with salt and black pepper to taste, and serve.

Simple Black Bean Soup

Serves 5-6

Ingredients:

1 cup dried black beans

5 cups vegetable broth

1 large onion, chopped

1 red pepper, chopped

1 tsp sweet paprika

1 tbsp dried mint

2 bay leaves

1 Serrano chili, finely chopped

1 tsp salt

4 tbsp fresh lime juice

1/2 cup chopped fresh cilantro

1 cup sour cream or yogurt, to serve

Directions:

Wash beans and soak them in enough water overnight.

In a slow cooker, combine the beans and all other ingredients except for the lime juice and cilantro. Cover and cook on low for 7-8 hours.

Add salt, lime juice and fresh cilantro.

Serve with a dollop of sour cream or yogurt.

Slow Cooker Minestrone

Serves 5-6

Ingredients:

4 bacon slices, chopped

1/2 onion, finely chopped

2 garlic cloves, crushed

1 carrot, peeled and diced

1 small red pepper, sliced

1 cup diced pumpkin

1 sweet potato, peeled and diced

1 zucchini, peeled and diced

4-5 white button mushrooms, sliced

5 cups vegetable broth

1 tsp dried oregano

1 tsp dried basil

salt and pepper, to taste

lemon juice, to serve

Directions:

Combine all ingredients in slow cooker.

Cover and cook on low for 3 hours.

Serve sprinkled with lemon juice

Heartwarming Split Pea Soup

Serves 5-6

Ingredients:

1 lb dried green split peas, rinsed and drained

2 potatoes, peeled and diced

1 small onion, chopped

1 celery rib, chopped

1 carrot, chopped

2 garlic cloves, chopped

1 bay leaf

1 tsp black pepper

1/2 tsp salt

6 cups water

Grated feta cheese, to serve

Directions:

Combine all ingredients in slow cooker.

Cover and cook on low for 5-6 hours.

Discard bay leaf. Blend soup to desired consistency, adding additional hot water to thin, if desired.

Sprinkle grated feta cheese on top and serve with garlic or herb bread.

Curried Lamb Shanks

Serves 4

Ingredients:

4 trimmed lamb shanks

2 tbsp plain flour

1 ½ lb spring potatoes

1 onion, thinly sliced

1/3 cup curry paste

1/2 cup pineapple juice

1 can coconut milk

1 cup chicken broth

½ tsp cinnamon

½ tsp black pepper

½ tsp salt

Directions:

Combine flour with salt, black pepper and cinnamon. Place this mixture together with shanks in a large snap-lock bag. Seal it and shake to coat well.

Spray the slow cooker with non stick spray.

Place the lamb shanks in it together with all other ingredients.

Cover and cook on low for 6-7 hours.

Slow Cooked Lamb with Red Wine Sauce

Serves 4

Ingredients:

4 trimmed lamb shanks

1 onion, thinly sliced

2 large carrots, roughly chopped

2-3 parsnips, roughly chopped

1 cup chicken broth

2 cups dry red wine

1 tsp brown sugar

½ tsp black pepper

½ tsp salt

Directions:

Spray the slow cooker with non stick spray.

Place the lamb shanks in it together with all other ingredients.

Cover and cook on low for 6-7 hours.

Lamb and Potato Casserole

Serves 4-5

Ingredients:

1 1/2 pounds shoulder lamb chops

12 small new potatoes, peeled, whole

3 onions, sliced

2 carrots, sliced

2 tbsp olive oil

2 tsp dried parsley

2 tsp dried mint

1/2 tsp pepper

1/2 tsp salt

Directions:

Spray the casserole with non stick spray. Place the lamb chops in it. Cover them with sliced onion, carrots, parsley, salt and pepper. Arrange new potatoes on and around the lamb. Add enough cold water to fill the dish halfway and season with mint, salt and pepper.

Cover and bake for 60 minutes in a preheated to 350 F oven.

Mediterranean Baked Fish

Serves 4

Ingredients:

1 ½ flounder or sole fillets

3 tomatoes, chopped

1/2 onion, chopped

2 cloves garlic, chopped

1/3 cup white wine

20 black olives, pitted and chopped

1 tbsp capers

3 tbsp Parmesan cheese

3 tbsp olive oil

1 tbsp fresh lemon juice

1 tsp dried oregano

4 leaves fresh basil, chopped

Directions:

Spray a casserole with non stick spray. Arrange the onion, garlic, oregano, tomatoes, wine, olives, capers, lemon juice and the chopped basil in it. Stir, add in Parmesan cheese, and top with the fish.

Bake in a preheated to 350 F oven for 30 minutes or until the fish is easily flaked with a fork.

Sweet and Sour Chicken

Serves 4

Ingredients:

4-5 chicken breasts

1 can baby corn

2 garlic cloves, crushed

1/4 cup soy sauce

1/4 cup maple syrup

3 tbsp ketchup

1 cup chicken broth

Directions:

Combine soy sauce, maple syrup, ketchup and garlic.

Place in slow cooker. Add chicken and baby corn and turn to coat. Add in chicken broth, cover, and cook on low for 4-5 hours.

Mediterranean Dump Chicken

Serves 4

Ingredients:

4-5 chicken breast halves

1 large onion, sliced

1 red bell pepper, thinly sliced

2 cups tomato pasta sauce

1/2 cup black olives, pitted

1/2 green olives, pitted

1/3 cup Parmesan cheese

1/2 cup chopped parsley

3 tbsp olive oil

salt and black pepper, to taste

Directions:

Place chicken breasts, onion, red pepper, pasta sauce and olives in a pan or cast iron skillet. Season with salt and pepper.

Cover and simmer 30-35 minutes. Sprinkle with Parmesan cheese and parsley and serve.

Blue Cheese and Mushroom Dump Chicken

Serves 4

Ingredients:

4 chicken breast halves

6-7 white button mushrooms, sliced

1 cup crumbled blue cheese

1/2 cup sour cream

salt and black pepper, to taste

1 cup walnuts, crushed, to serve

Directions:

Heat oven to 350 degrees F. Spray a casserole with non stick spray. Place all ingredients into it, turn chicken to coat.

Bake until chicken juices run clear. Sprinkle with walnuts and serve.

Slow Cooker Paprika Chicken

Serves 4

Ingredients:

8 chicken drumsticks

1 onion, chopped

2 slices bacon, finely chopped

1 large red pepper, chopped

1 large green pepper

2 garlic cloves, finely chopped

1 tbsp paprika

1 can crushed tomatoes

2 cups chicken broth

1/2 cup medium-grain white rice

1 tbsp sour cream

1/2 cup fresh parsley, finely cut, to serve

Directions:

Combine all ingredients in Crockpot.

Cover and cook on low for 5-6 hours.

Pesto Chicken

Serves 4

Ingredients:

5-6 chicken breast halves

1 small jar pesto sauce

1 cup sour cream

Directions:

Spray the slow cooker with non stick spray.

Dump all ingredients into slow cooker and turn chicken to coat well.

Cook on low for 5-6 hours.

Pineapple Chicken

Serves 4

Ingredients:

4-5 chicken breast halves

1 small red onion, finely cut

1 cup pineapple chunks

1 cup pineapple juice

1 tsp lime zest

1 tbsp soy sauce

1/2 tsp grated ginger

1/2 cup golden raisins

Directions:

Spray the slow cooker with non stick spray.

Dump all ingredients into slow cooker and turn chicken to coat.

Cook on low for 5-6 hours.

Garlicky Lime Chicken

Serves 4

Ingredients:

4-5 chicken breast halves

2 garlic cloves, crushed

1 red pepper, thinly sliced

1/2 can sweet corn

1/4 cup lime juice

1/2 tsp lime zest

½ crushed coriander seeds

½ tsp hot paprika

1 tsp black pepper

1/4 tsp salt

Directions:

Preheat the oven to 350 F. Spray a casserole with non stick spray.

Place all ingredients into the casserole and turn chicken to coat.

Bake for about 40 minutes or until chicken juices run clear.

Peanut Butter Dump Chicken

Serves 4

Ingredients:

4-5 chicken breast halves, cut in 1 inch pieces

3-4 green onions, finely cut

4-5 white button mushrooms, sliced

¾ cup smooth peanut butter

1 tbsp soy sauce

Directions:

Preheat oven to 350 F.

Spray a casserole with non stick spray.

Place all ingredients into the casserole and turn chicken to coat.

Bake for about 40 minutes or until chicken juices run clear.

Dump Chicken and Potatoes

Serves 4

Ingredients:

4 skinless, boneless chicken breast halves or 4-5 chicken tights

12 oz new potatoes

1 onion, sliced

2 carrots, cut

1 red bell pepper, halved, deseeded, cut

1 zucchini, peeled and cut in 1-2 inch pieces

4 garlic cloves, halved

1 cup water

1 tsp dried oregano

salt and pepper, to taste

Directions:

Spray the casserole with non stick spray. Place the chicken in it. Add all vegetables around the chicken. Season with salt and pepper, to taste.

Sprinkle with oregano, add in water, and bake, uncovered, at 350 F for 45 minutes.

Chicken Drumstick Casserole

Serves 4

Ingredients:

8 chicken drumsticks

1 leek, trimmed, thinly sliced

2 garlic cloves, crushed

1 cup tomatoes, diced

1 cup black olives, pitted

1 cup canned chickpeas, drained and rinsed

1 tsp dried rosemary

salt and black pepper, to taste

Directions:

Spray a casserole with non stick spray. Dump all ingredients in it and turn the chicken to coat well.

Bake at 350 F until chicken juices run clear, about 40-45 minutes

Season with salt and pepper to taste and serve.

Greek Chicken Casserole

Serves 5-6

Ingredients:

4-5 skinless, boneless chicken breast halves or 8 tights

1 lb potatoes, peeled and cubed

1 lb green beans, trimmed and cut in 1 inch pieces

1 large onion, chopped

2 cups diced, canned tomatoes, undrained

5 cloves garlic, minced

1 cup feta cheese, crumbled

salt and black pepper, to taste

Directions:

Spray a casserole with non stick spray. Dump the chicken, onion, thyme, black pepper and garlic in it and stir to coat well.

Add in potatoes, green beans and tomatoes, season with salt and pepper to taste, and top with crumbled feta.

Bake in a preheated to 350 F oven for 40-45 minutes.

Chicken with Almonds and Prunes

Serves 4

Ingredients:

1.5 lb chicken thigh fillets

1/3 cup fresh orange juice

2 tbsp honey

1/3 cup white wine

1/2 cup pitted prunes

2 tbsp blanched almonds

2 tbsp raisins or sultanas

1 tsp ground cinnamon

salt and black pepper, to taste

1/2 cup fresh parsley leaves, chopped, to serve

Directions:

Place the chicken pieces, orange juice, wine, honey, prunes, almonds, raisins and cinnamon in a pan or iron skillet.

Bring to a boil, reduce heat to medium, and simmer 35-40 minutes, or until chicken is just tender. Season to taste with salt and pepper, sprinkle with parsley and serve.

Easy Chicken Parmigiana

Serves 4

Ingredients:

4 chicken breast halves

1 eggplant, peeled and sliced lengthwise

1 can tomatoes, diced

9 oz mozzarella cheese, sliced

Directions:

Spray a casserole with non stick spray. Add the chicken pieces. Place eggplant over the chicken and add in tomatoes.

Top with mozzarella slices and bake in a preheated to 350 F for 30-35 minutes.

One-Pot Chicken Dijonnaise

Serves 4

Ingredients:

4 chicken breast halves with skin

1 onion, sliced

5-6 white button mushrooms, sliced

2 garlic cloves, crushed

1/3 cup Dijon mustard

1/3 cup mayonnaise

1/3 cup dry white wine

1/2 cup sour cream

2 tbsp finely chopped tarragon

salt and pepper, to taste

Directions:

Spray a casserole with non stick spray. Add the chicken, onion, mushrooms and garlic.

In a small bowl, combine wine, mayonnaise, Dijon mustard, sour cream and tarragon. Pour this mixture over the chicken. Season with salt and black pepper to taste

Bake in a preheated to 350 F oven for 30 minutes or until chicken is cooked through and the liquid has evaporated.

Sweet and Sour Sicilian Chicken

Serves 4

Ingredients:

4 chicken thigh fillets

1 large red onion, sliced

3 garlic cloves, chopped

2 tbsp flour

1/3 cup dry white wine

1 cup chicken broth

1/2 cup green olives

2 tbsp olive oil

2 bay leaves

1 tbsp fresh oregano leaves

2 tbsp brown sugar or honey

2 tbsp red wine vinegar

salt and black pepper, to taste

Directions:

Combine the flour with salt and black pepper and coat well the chicken pieces.

Spray a casserole with non stick spray and place the chicken in it. Add in onion, garlic, wine, the chicken broth, olives, bay leaves, oregano, sugar and vinegar.

Bake, in a preheated to 380 F oven, for 35 minutes, or until the chicken is cooked through.

Lemon Rosemary Chicken

Serves 4

Ingredients:

4 boneless skinless chicken breasts or 4-5 tights

2 garlic cloves, crushed

4-5 lemon slices

4-5 black olives, pitted

1 tbsp capers

1 tbsp dried rosemary

3 tbsp olive oil

salt and pepper, to taste

Directions:

Place the lemon slices at the bottom of a skillet and lay the chicken breasts on top of the lemon. Add in olives, rosemary, capers, salt and pepper to taste.

Cover, and cook, on medium-low, for 35-40 minutes or until the chicken is cooked through.

Uncover and cook for 2-3 minutes, until the liquid evaporates.

Easy Beef Crock Pot

Serves 4

Ingredients:

2 lbs beef, cubed

1 small onion, finely cut

1 celery rib, finely cut

1 can cream of mushrooms soup

½ cup water or vegetable broth

Directions:

Spray the slow cooker with non stick spray.

Combine all ingredients into the slow cooker, cover, and cook on low for 7-9 hours.

Beef and Pumpkin Stew

Serves 4-5

Ingredients:

2 lbs lean beef, cubed

2 cups cubed pumpkin

1 small onion, chopped

2 garlic cloves, chopped

1 tomato, diced

zest of one orange

1 bay leaf

1 tsp paprika

4 tbsp olive oil

salt and black pepper, to taste

3 green onions, chopped, to serve

Directions:

In a stew pot, add all ingredients with enough water to cover everything.

Bring to a boil, reduce heat to low, cover, and simmer for 60-65 minutes, or until the beef is cooked through.

Sprinkle with green onions and serve.

Beef and Onion Crock Pot

Serves 6

Ingredients:

2 lbs lean beef, cubed

3 lbs shallots, peeled

5 garlic cloves, peeled, whole

3 tbsp tomato paste, dissolved in 1/3 cup water

1 bay leaf

3 tbsp red wine vinegar

1 tsp salt

2 cups beef or chicken broth

Directions:

Combine all ingredients in Crockpot. Cover and cook on low for 7-9 hours.

Beef and Green Pea Crock Pot

Serves 6

Ingredients:

2 lbs stewing beef

2 bags(10 oz each) frozen peas

1 onion, chopped

3-4 garlic cloves, cut

1 carrot, chopped

1 cup chicken or beef broth

1 tsp salt

1 tbsp paprika

1/2 cup fresh dill, finely chopped

1 cup yogurt, to serve

Directions:

Combine all ingredients in Crockpot. Cover and cook on low for 6 hours. Serve sprinkled with fresh dill and a dollop of yogurt.

Beef and Root Vegetable Crock Pot

Serves 6

Ingredients:

2 lbs stewing beef

2 carrots, cut

2 onions, sliced

1 small turnip, peeled and diced

1 small beet, peeled and diced

1 cup beef broth

1 tsp tomato paste

1 tbsp paprika

2 bay leaves

1 cup yogurt, to serve

Directions:

Combine all ingredients in Crockpot. Cover and cook on low for 6 hours.

Slow Cooked Mediterranean Beef

Serves 6

Ingredients:

2 lb lean steak, cut into large pieces

3 onions, sliced

4 garlic cloves, cut

1 red pepper, cut

1 green pepper, cut

1 bag frozen green beans

1 zucchini, peeled and cut

tomato, diced

2 tbsp tomato paste or purée

1/2 cup dry red wine

1 cup water or chicken broth

1 tsp dried oregano

salt and black pepper, to taste

Directions:

Combine all ingredients in Crockpot. Cover and cook on low for 6 hours.

Serve with mashed potatoes or couscous.

Beef Stew with Quince

Serves 6-8

Ingredients:

2 lbs chuck roast, cut into 2 inch pieces

2 onions, chopped

2-3 tomatoes, pureed

1-2 bay leaves

1 cinnamon stick

1 cup dry white wine

3 quinces, peeled, cored and cubed

5-6 prunes

1 tsp paprika

1 tsp salt

1/2 tsp black pepper

1 tbsp honey

6 tbsp olive oil

Directions:

Place the beef and the onions in a stewing pot. Add in the quince, prunes, honey, wine, bay leaves, cinnamon, tomato puree, salt, pepper, and enough water to cover the meat. Stir, cover, and bring to a simmer.

Cook for 60-80 minutes.

Before serving discard the bay leaves and the cinnamon stick.

Sausage and Beans

Serves 4

Ingredients:

1 lb lean smoked turkey sausage, cut into 1-inch slices

1 big onion, finely cut

2 garlic cloves, crushed

1 can white or black beans, undrained

1 can diced tomatoes

1 tbsp dried mint

1/2 cup finely cut parsley, to serve

Directions:

Place sausages, onions, and garlic in a skillet or pan. Add in beans, tomatoes and mint.

Stir, cover, and simmer for 20 minutes or until the sauce is thick. Serve sprinkled with fresh parsley.

Turkey Sausage and Lentil One-pot

Serves 4

Ingredients:

1 lb lean smoked turkey sausage, cut into 1-inch slices

1 big onion, chopped

2 garlic cloves, crushed

1 red pepper, sliced

1 cup green lentils, rinsed

1 cup vegetable broth

1 tbsp dried mint

1/2 cup finely cut parsley, to serve

Directions:

Place sausages, onions, garlic and red pepper in a pot. Add in lentils, vegetable broth and mint.

Stir, cover, and simmer for for 20 min until lentils have softened and sausages are cooked through. Serve sprinkled with fresh parsley.

Slow Cooked Pot Roast

Serves 4

Ingredients:

2 lb pot roast

2 garlic cloves, crushed

1 onion, finely cut

1/2 cup tomato paste

1/2 cup chicken broth

1 tbsp Worcestershire sauce

1 tsp salt

Directions:

Spray the slow cooker with non stick spray.

Sprinkle salt over the roast and place in the slow cooker.

In a bowl, combine the tomato paste, chicken broth, Worcestershire sauce, garlic, and onions. Spread this mixture over meat.

Cover and cook on low 8-10 hours.

Mediterranean Pork Casserole

Serves 4

Ingredients:

1 1/2 lb pork loin, cut into cubes

1 large onion, chopped

1 cup white button mushrooms, cut

2 garlic cloves, finely chopped

1 green pepper, deseeded and cut into strips

1 small eggplant, peeled and diced

1 zucchini, peeled and diced

2 tomatoes, chopped

½ cup chicken broth

1 tsp summer savory

1 tbsp paprika

salt and black pepper, to taste

Directions:

Place all ingredients in a stewing pot. Cover and simmer for 40-60 minutes or until the pork is tender.

Uncover, and cook for 5 minutes more. Serve with mashed potatoes or rice pilaf.

Pork Roast and Cabbage

Serves 4

Ingredients:

2 cups cooked pork roast, chopped

1/2 head cabbage

1/2 onion, chopped

1 lemon, juice only

1 tomato, diced

2 tbsp olive oil

1 tsp paprika

1/2 tsp cumin

salt and black pepper, to taste

Directions:

In an ovenproof casserole dish, heat olive oil and gently sauté cabbage, pork and onions for a minute, stirring. Add in cumin, paprika, lemon juice and tomato.

Cover and bake at 350 F for 20-25 minutes, or until vegetables are tender.

Orange Pork Chops

Serves 4

Ingredients:

4 pork chops, about 4 oz each

1 onion, thinly sliced

4 garlic cloves, crushed

3 tbsp olive oil

1/4 tsp cumin

1/2 tsp dried oregano

1 tsp black pepper

1 tbsp raw honey

1 cup orange juice

Directions:

Crush the garlic, oregano, black pepper and cumin together into a paste. Rub each chop with the garlic paste and arrange them in a casserole dish.

Dilute one tablespoon of honey into the orange juice and pour it over the chops. Add in onions.

Bake in a preheated to 350 F on for 45 minutes, or until the chops are cooked through.

Juicy Pork Chops

Serves 4

Ingredients:

4-5 pork chops, about 4 oz each

4 garlic cloves, crushed

1 tbsp honey

3 tbsp olive oil

1 tbsp vinegar

1/2 cup white wine

1 tbsp soy sauce

1 tbsp ketchup

1/2 tsp dried sage

1 tsp black pepper

1/2 tsp salt

Directions:

In a cup, combine all liquid ingredients and stir until very well mixed. Crush the garlic, sage, black pepper and salt together into a paste. Rub each chop with the garlic paste and arrange them in a casserole dish.

Pour the liquid mix over the chops. Cover the casserole and bake in a preheated to 350 F on for 45 minutes, or until the chops are cooked through.

Pork and Peanut Butter Curry

Serves 4

Ingredients:

1 lb pork tenderloin, sliced

5-6 green onions, finely cut

1 can baby corn

4 tbsp Thai red curry paste

1/3 cup crunchy peanut butter

1 tbsp brown sugar

1 tbsp soy sauce

1 can light coconut milk

½ cup fresh coriander, finely cut

3 tbsp lime juice

Directions:

Spray the slow cooker with non stick spray.

Combine all ingredients into the slow cooker. Cover, and cook on low for 7-9 hours.

Pork and Mushroom Crock Pot

Serves 4

Ingredients:

2 lbs pork tenderloin, sliced

2 cups chopped white button mushrooms

1 can cream of mushroom soup

½ cup sour cream

1/2 tsp black pepper

1/2 tsp salt

Directions:

Spray the slow cooker with non stick spray.

Combine all ingredients into the slow cooker. Cover, and cook on low for 7-9 hours.

Potato and Zucchini Bake

Serves 6

Ingredients:

1½ lb potatoes, peeled and sliced into rounds

5 zucchinis, peeled and sliced into rounds

2 onions, sliced

3 tomatoes, pureed

½ cup water

4 tbsp olive oil

1 tsp dried oregano

1/3 cup fresh parsley leaves, chopped

salt and black pepper, to taste

Directions:

Place potatoes, zucchinis and onions in a large, shallow ovenproof baking dish. Pour over the olive oil and pureed tomatoes. Add salt and freshly ground pepper to taste and toss the everything together. Add in water.

Bake in a preheated to 350 F oven for 45 minutes, stirring halfway through.

Spicy Quinoa Crock Pot

Serves 4

Ingredients:

1 can black beans, drained and rinsed

1 can sweet corn, drained and rinsed

1 cup quinoa, rinsed

2 cans tomato sauce

1 cup vegetable broth

3-4 garlic cloves, crushed

2 tbsp pickled jalapeños

4 oz cream cheese

1 tsp cumin

1 tsp dried oregano

salt and pepper, to taste

½ cup cilantro chopped

1 cup sour cream

Directions:

Spray the slow cooker with non stick spray.

Combine all ingredients into the slow cooker, except for the cilantro and sour cream.

Cover and cook on low for 5-6 hours.

Uncover, top with sour cream and chopped cilantro and serve.

Slow Cooker Sweet Potato and Chickpea Chili

Serves 4

Ingredients:

1 can chickpeas, drained and rinsed

1 can tomatoes, diced, undrained

1 large sweet potato, peeled and cut into 2 inch cubes

2 onions, chopped

2 carrots, peeled and diced

1 green pepper, chopped

1 cup vegetable broth

1 tsp garlic powder

2 tbsp chili powder

1 tbsp paprika

1 tsp cumin

salt and black pepper, to taste

4-5 green onions, finely cut, to serve

1 avocado, pitted, peeled and diced, to serve

1 cup yogurt, to serve

Directions:

Spray the slow cooker with non stick spray.

Combine all ingredients into the slow cooker.

Cover and cook on low for 6-7 hours.

Uncover, top with yogurt, avocado and green onions, and serve.

Green Pea and Mushroom Stew

Serves 4

Ingredients:

1 bag frozen peas

5 large white button mushrooms, sliced

3-4 green onions, chopped

1 large carrot, chopped

1-2 cloves garlic

1/2 cup water

1/2 cup finely chopped dill

salt and black pepper, to taste

Directions:

In a stew pot, combine green peas, mushrooms, carrot, green onions, garlic, and water.

Bring to a boil, cover, and simmer for 20-25 minutes. When ready sprinkle with dill and serve.

Potato and Leek Stew

Serves 4

Ingredients:

12 oz potatoes, diced

2-3 leeks cut into thick rings

5-6 tbsp olive oil

1 cup water

1/2 cup finely cut parsley

1 tsp paprika

salt and black pepper, to taste

Directions:

Heat olive oil in a heavy wide saucepan or sauté pan. Add in leeks, paprika, salt and pepper, and sauté for 2-3 minutes, stirring. Add in potatoes and water. The water should cover the vegetables.

Bring to a boil and simmer until all vegetables are tender. Sprinkle with finely chopped parsley and serve.

Baked Bean and Rice Casserole

Serves 4

Ingredients

1 15 oz can white or red beans, drained

1/2 cup rice, rinsed

1 cup vegetable broth

½ bunch parsley, finely cut

1 tbsp dried mint

½ tsp black pepper

1 tsp salt

Directions:

In a deep ovenproof casserole, combine beans, rice and vegetable broth.

Add in mint, parsley, salt and pepper to taste, and bake in a preheated to 350 F oven for 20 minutes.

Creamy Green Pea and Rice Casserole

Serves 4

Ingredients

1 onion, very finely cut

1 bag frozen peas

2-3 garlic cloves, chopped

3-4 mushrooms, chopped

1/2 cup white rice

1 cup water

4 tbsp olive oil

1/2 cup sour cream

2/3 cup grated Parmesan cheese

1/2 cup fresh dill, finely cut

salt and black pepper, to taste

Directions:

Spray a casserole with non stick spray. Add the onions, garlic, mushrooms, rice and frozen peas. Stir in water and dill.

Bake in a preheated to 350 F oven, for 20 minutes.

Stir in sour cream, sprinkle with Parmesan cheese, bake for 2-3 more minutes and serve.

Eggplant Casserole

Serves 4

Ingredients:

2 medium eggplants, peeled and diced

1 cup canned tomatoes, drained and diced

1 zucchini, peeled and diced

9-10 black olives, pitted

1 onion, chopped

4 garlic cloves, chopped

2 tbsp tomato paste

salt and black pepper, to taste

1 cup parsley, chopped, to serve

Directions:

Spray a casserole with non stick spray and place all ingredients inside. Stir to combine.

Bake at 350 F for 30-40 minutes. Sprinkle with parsley and serve.

Green Bean and Potato Stew

Serves 5-6

Ingredients:

2 cups green beans, fresh or frozen

2 onions, chopped

3-4 potatoes, peeled and diced

2 carrots, cut

4 cloves garlic, crushed

1 cup fresh parsley, chopped

1/2 cup fresh dill, finely chopped

4 tbsp olive oil

1/2 cup water

2 tsp tomato paste

salt and pepper, to taste

Directions:

In a large casserole, mix together onion, garlic, green beans and the remaining ingredients.

Cover, bring to a gentle boil and simmer over medium heat for about an hour or until all vegetables are tender.

Serve sprinkled with fresh dill.

Okra and Tomato Casserole

Serves 4-5

Ingredients:

1 lb okra, stem ends trimmed

4 large tomatoes, cut into wedges

3 garlic cloves, chopped

3 tbsp olive oil

1 tsp salt

black pepper, to taste

Directions:

In a large casserole, mix together trimmed okra, sliced tomatoes, olive oil and chopped garlic. Add salt and pepper and toss to combine.

Bake in a preheated to 350 F oven for 45 minutes, or until the okra is tender.

FREE BONUS RECIPES: 10 Ridiculously Easy Jam and Jelly Recipes Anyone Can Make

A Different Strawberry Jam

Makes 6-7 11 oz jars

Ingredients:

4 lb fresh small strawberries (stemmed and cleaned)

5 cups sugar

1 cup water

2 tbsp lemon juice or 1 tsp citric acid

Directions:

Mix water and sugar and bring to the boil. Simmer sugar syrup for 5-6 minutes then slowly drop in the cleaned strawberries. Stir and bring to the boil again. Lower heat and simmer, stirring and skimming any foam off the top once or twice.

Drop a small amount of the jam on a plate and wait a minute to see if it has thickened. If it has gelled enough, turn off the heat. If not, keep boiling and test every 5 minutes until ready. Two or three minutes before you remove the jam from the heat, add lemon juice or citric acid and stir well.

Ladle the hot jam in the jars until 1/8-inch from the top. Place the lid on top and flip the jar upside down. Continue until all of the jars are filled and upside down. Allow the jam to cool completely before turning right-side up. Press on the lid to check and see if it has sealed. If one of the jars lids doesn't pop up- the jar is not sealed–store it in a refrigerator.

Raspberry Jam

Makes 4-5 11 oz jars

Ingredients:

4 cups raspberries

4 cups sugar

1 tsp vanilla extract

1/2 tsp citric acid

Directions:

Gently wash and drain the raspberries. Lightly crush them with a potato masher, food mill or a food processor. Do not puree, it is better to have bits of fruit. Sieve half of the raspberry pulp to remove some of the seeds. Combine sugar and raspberries in a wide, thick-bottomed pot and bring mixture to a full rolling boil, stirring constantly. Skim any scum or foam that rises to the surface. Boil until the jam sets.

Test by putting a small drop on a cold plate – if the jam is set, it will wrinkle when given a small poke with your finger. Add citric acid, vanilla, and stir. Simmer for 2-3 minutes more, then ladle into hot jars. Flip upside down or process 10 minutes in boiling water.

Raspberry-Peach Jam

Makes 4-5 11 oz jars

Ingredients:

2 lb peaches

1 1/2 cup raspberries

4 cups sugar

1 tsp citric acid

Directions:

Wash and slice the peaches. Clean the raspberries and combine them with the peaches is a wide, heavy-bottomed saucepan. Cover with sugar and set aside for a few hours or overnight. Bring the fruit and sugar to a boil over medium heat, stirring occasionally. Remove any foam that rises to the surface.

Boil until the jam sets. Add citric acid and stir. Simmer for 2-3 minutes more, then ladle into hot jars. Flip upside down or process 10 minutes in boiling water.

Blueberry Jam

Makes 4-5 11 oz jars

Ingredients:

4 cups granulated sugar

3 cups blueberries (frozen and thawed or fresh)

3/4 cup honey

2 tbsp lemon juice

1 tsp lemon zest

Directions:

Gently wash and drain the blueberries. Lightly crush them with a potato masher, food mill or a food processor. Add the honey, lemon juice, and lemon zest, then bring to a boil over medium-high heat. Boils for 10-15 minutes, stirring from time to time. Boil until the jam sets.

Test by putting a small drop on a cold plate – if the jam is set, it will wrinkle when given a small poke with your finger. Skim off any foam, then ladle the jam into jars. Seal, flip upside down or process for 10 minutes in boiling water.

Triple Berry Jam

Makes 4-5 11 oz jars

Ingredients:

1 cup strawberries

1 cup raspberries

2 cups blueberries

4 cups sugar

1 tsp citric acid

Directions:

Mix berries and add sugar. Set aside for a few hours or overnight. Bring the fruit and sugar to the boil over medium heat, stirring frequently. Remove any foam that rises to the surface. Boil until the jam sets. Add citric acid, salt and stir.

Simmer for 2-3 minutes more, then ladle into hot jars. Flip upside down or process 10 minutes in boiling water.

Red Currant Jelly

Makes 6-7 11 oz jars

Ingredients:

2 lb fresh red currants

1/2 cup water

3 cups sugar

1 tsp citric acid

Directions:

Place the currants into a large pot, and crush with a potato masher or berry crusher. Add in water, and bring to a boil. Simmer for 10 minutes. Strain the fruit through a jelly or cheese cloth and measure out 4 cups of the juice. Pour the juice into a large saucepan, and stir in the sugar.

Bring to full rolling boil, then simmer for 20-30 minutes, removing any foam that may rise to the surface. When the jelly sets, ladle in hot jars, flip upside down or process in boiling water for 10 minutes.

White Cherry Jam

Makes 3-4 11 oz jars

Ingredients:

2 lb cherries

3 cups sugar

2 cups water

1 tsp citric acid

Directions:

Wash and stone cherries. Combine water and sugar and bring to the boil. Boil for 5-6 minutes then remove from heat and add cherries. Bring to a rolling boil and cook until set. Add citric acid, stir and boil 1-2 minutes more.

Ladle in hot jars, flip upside down or process in boiling water for 10 minutes.

Cherry Jam

Makes 3-4 11 oz jars

Ingredients:

2 lb fresh cherries, pitted, halved

4 cups sugar

1/2 cup lemon juice

Directions:

Place the cherries in a large saucepan. Add sugar and set aside for an hour. Add the lemon juice and place over low heat. Cook, stirring occasionally, for 10 minutes or until sugar dissolves. Increase heat to high and bring to a rolling boil.

Cook for 5-6 minutes or until jam is set. Remove from heat and ladle hot jam into jars, seal and flip upside down.

Oven Baked Ripe Fig Jam

Makes 3-4 11 oz jars

Ingredients:

2 lb ripe figs

2 cups sugar

1 ½ cups water

2 tbsp lemon juice

Directions:

Arrange the figs in a Dutch oven, if they are very big, cut them in halves. Add sugar and water and stir well. Bake at 350 F for about one and a half hours. Do not stir. You can check the readiness by dropping a drop of the syrup in a cup of cold water – if it falls to the bottom without dissolving, the jam is ready. If the drop dissolves before falling, you can bake it a little longer. Take out of the oven, add lemon juice and ladle in the warm jars. Place the lids on top and flip the jars upside down. Allow the jam to cool completely before turning right-side up.

If you want to process the jams - place them into a large pot, cover the jars with water by at least 2 inches and bring to a boil. Boil for 10 minutes, remove the jars and sit to cool.

Quince Jam

Makes 5-6 11 oz jars

Ingredients:

4 lb quinces

5 cups sugar

2 cups water

1 tsp lemon zest

3 tbsp lemon juice

Directions:

Combine water and sugar in a deep, thick-bottomed saucepan and bring it to the boil. Simmer, stirring until the sugar has completely dissolved. Rinse the quinces, cut in half, and discard the cores. Grate the quinces, using a cheese grater or a blender to make it faster. Quince flesh tends to darken very quickly, so it is good to do this as fast as possible.

Add the grated quinces to the sugar syrup and cook uncovered, stirring occasionally until the jam turns pink and thickens to desired consistency, about 40 minutes.

Drop a small amount of the jam on a plate and wait a minute to see if it has thickened. If it has gelled enough, turn off the heat. If not, keep boiling and test every 2-3 minutes until ready. Two or three minutes before you remove the jam from the heat, add lemon juice and lemon zest and stir well.

Ladle in hot, sterilized jars and flip upside down.

About the Author

Vesela lives in Bulgaria with her family of six (including the Jack Russell Terrier). Her passion is going green in everyday life and she loves to prepare homemade cosmetic and beauty products for all her family and friends.

Vesela has been publishing her cookbooks for over a year now. If you want to see other healthy family recipes that she has published, together with some natural beauty books, you can check out her Author Page on Amazon.

22492115R00042

Printed in Great Britain
by Amazon